The
Van Gogh
Cafe

OTHER HARCOURT BOOKS BY CYNTHIA RYLANT

Ludie's Life

Boris

Gooseberry Park

I Had Seen Castles

Something Permanent

CYNTHIA RYLANT

The Van Gogh Cafe

DEVELOPMENTAL STUDIES CENTER

This Developmental Studies Center edition is published by arrangement
with Houghton Mifflin Harcourt Publishing Company.

Developmental Studies Center
1250 53rd Street, Suite 3
Emeryville, CA 94608-2965
800.666.7270 ⋆ fax: 510.464.3670
devstu.org

The text was set in Spectrum
Designed by Linda Lockowitz

Cover photographs (*café*) © Brendan Regan/Corbis,
(*stars*) © Heather Perry/Getty, (*butterflies*) © Gary Carter/Corbis,
(*café sign*) © Veer
Cover design by Jennifer Jackman

ISBN 978-1-61003-500-2
Printed in China

1 2 3 4 5 6 7 8 9 10 RRD 22 21 20 19 18 17 16 15 14

To Dav,
for seven years of magic

The
Van Gogh
Cafe

The Cafe

THE VAN GOGH CAFE sits on Main Street in Flowers, Kansas, and the building it is in was once a theater, which may be the reason for its magic. Anyone who has ever seen anything happen on a stage—anything— knows that a theater is so full of magic that after years and years of opening nights there must be magic enough to last forever in its walls. The Van Gogh Cafe is lucky it hasn't found itself in a building where people perhaps once had their broken arms fixed or their teeth pulled out.

Those are not the sort of walls that harbor magic. But theater walls do.

Magic is a powerful word and often misused. Some say magic comes from heaven, and others say it comes from hell, but anyone who has ever visited the Van Gogh Cafe knows that magic comes from a building that was once a theater; from a sign above a cash register that reads BLESS ALL DOGS; from a smiling porcelain hen on top of a pie carousel; from purple hydrangeas painted all over a ladies' bathroom; from a small brown phonograph that plays "You'd Be So Nice to Come Home To." Magic is in the Van Gogh Cafe in Flowers, Kansas, and sometimes the magic wakes itself up, and people and animals and things notice it. They notice it and are affected by it and pretty soon word spreads that there is a cafe—the Van Gogh Cafe—that is wonderful, like a dream, like a mystery, like a painting, and you ought to go there, they will say, for you will never forget it. You will want to stay, if you can. Some have for a while. Like the possum . . .

The Possum

KANSAS IS NOT what one would call picturesque. It is flat. So flat it could make some people a little crazy, people who need a hill now and then to keep their balance. But in Kansas at least things get noticed. The flatness makes everything count and not one thing slips by. That is why, if a possum was going to choose to hang upside down somewhere, Kansas would be a good choice. People would notice. And if the possum chose to hang outside the window of the Van Gogh Cafe in

Flowers . . . well then, everyone would start talking about magic. And that would be good for the possum, too.

The Van Gogh Cafe is owned by a young man named Marc and his daughter, Clara. Clara is one reason for all of the magic in the cafe. She is ten and believes anything might happen.

Marc bought the cafe seven years ago, and he is the one who painted purple hydrangeas all over the ladies' bathroom and put the sign above the cash register. But the phonograph and the hen were already there when he arrived. Clara's mother doesn't like Kansas and she lives in New York City, where Clara visits her each June. But Clara preferred Kansas the moment she laid eyes on it. Kansas is like a tall person relaxing, she says. It seems right for her.

Marc and Clara open up the cafe at six every morning except Sundays, when they sleep until ten. Clara takes breakfast orders for Marc—who is the cook—for half an hour on school mornings, then she goes to their apartment across the street to get ready for school. Clara likes taking orders because everyone is sleepy and sweet and all they want in the world is a cup of coffee, please. Clara thinks morning is the kindest time of day.

Most of the people who come to the Van Gogh Cafe are Flowers people and know each other: "Hi, Ray." "Hello, Roy." But sometimes someone is new, for Flowers sits near I-70, which people take when they are escaping from an old life in the East to a new life in the West or the other way around. Clara has met many people between six and six-thirty on their way to something new.

But she has not met a possum until today. Today is Saturday and she's working a couple extra hours for her father, and it is eight o'clock in the morning when suddenly a possum is hanging upside down in the tree outside the cafe window. Right on Main Street. A minute ago it wasn't there and now it is.

Clara sees it first: *Look, there's a possum.* Coffee cups go down, heads turn, and outside a little gray possum enjoys being noticed. It scratches its nose and blinks its eyes and stares back at all the faces.

No one sitting down can say hello to a possum. So everyone in the cafe gets up and stands in front of the window. Now, this is the magic of the Van Gogh Cafe: not one person says, "Amazing! A possum upside down on Main Street!" No, everyone is not all that surprised. They, like Clara, have come to believe anything might happen, because they have been having breakfast at the Van Gogh Cafe all their lives.

What they *do* say is, "Hi." Many of them wave. Ray asks Roy what possums eat. And, with their usual curiosity about every new person in

Flowers, they all say, "Wonder where he's from?"

Well, it's hard to know a possum's story before he does something magical, but after he does, there's story and more to tell.

One of the first stories is that the possum starts coming back to the Van Gogh Cafe every day. Eight in the morning, he's up in the tree.

But that's a small story.

The possum begins to attract people, and this is the bigger story because he attracts people who haven't been getting along. Best friends who had a fight the day before: today they're standing on the sidewalk next to the possum. The possum is hanging upside down and blinking, and the two friends are talking, and suddenly they've got their arms around each other and are coming into the cafe for some pie.

A young husband and wife: the day before they're yelling in the front yard, the next day they're kissing beside the possum.

Two neighbors: the day before they're arguing about loud music, the next day the possum is watching them shake hands.

The story becomes even bigger when people start bringing food out of the Van Gogh Cafe, food for the possum. Half an English muffin here, two pieces of oven-fried potatoes there, a cup of milk. They can't help themselves; they want to give it some food.

The possum isn't hungry. But a stray dog from the other end of town is, and he starts stopping by for breakfast. So does a thin cat and two baby kittens. And a shy small mouse. Several sparrows. Even a deer.

And this goes on for a while until the biggest story happens. A story that will enter quietly into the walls of the cafe and become part of its magic.

For a man whose wife has died drives

through Flowers, Kansas, one morning on his way to something new. He is sad. He really isn't sure where he's going.

But passing the Van Gogh Cafe, he sees the possum. He sees the possum and he sees all the hungry animals standing beneath it, eating the scraps of muffins and potatoes.

And the man sees something else there, too, something no one has seen until now. And because of what he sees, he turns his car around and drives back where he belongs, back to his farm, which he turns into a home for stray animals, animals who come to him and take away his loneliness.

Since that day the possum at the Van Gogh Cafe has disappeared. One minute it was there, the next minute it wasn't.

But the customers still bring food out of the cafe every morning, leaving scraps beneath the tree in case anyone hungry happens by.

There is always a new stray dog, a new thin cat, sparrows.

Clara is not surprised the possum has gone away. Things are always changing at the Van Gogh Cafe, and something new is sure to happen soon. Perhaps when lightning strikes . . .

Lightning Strikes

AFTER LIGHTNING struck the Van Gogh Cafe one day in March, the soup didn't need to be heated for a week. You could just open up a can and the soup would be steaming.

Now it is April and the lightning is still having an effect: everything Marc cooks is coming out perfect. Perfect. Not one burnt crust, not one overcooked egg, everything has just enough salt the first time. Perfect.

The effect of this has not been lost on Marc, who has taken to writing poetry while he cooks.

Clara and Marc were both at the cafe when the lightning struck. In fact, they were closing up for the night. Marc had the key in the door and they were just getting ready to step out into the rain when a blinding light flashed, the cafe popped, and the key in Marc's hand melted inside the lock. But that was the only damage. Odd . . . but, of course, this is the Van Gogh Cafe.

Since then, things have been a little tipped, a little to one side, here at the cafe. The hen's smile is a bit crooked. The sign above the register won't stay straight. People come in and their hats fall off.

Clara knows it is because of the lightning. And she knows this won't last, that everything will straighten up again.

But she expects something larger to happen before everyone's hats begin staying on their heads. She expects a bigger story.

Naturally, one comes.

The smaller story began with the perfect food Marc was cooking. But this could have been just luck. Perfect food doesn't have to involve magic.

However, food that cooks itself does.

Marc is thinking of nothing else but poetry. A month ago he wasn't a poet. Now he is. He is a little crazy with writing, and since the food he's cooking has been so perfect lately, he is starting to forget it altogether. He is forgetting to flip the eggs off the grill, to pull the toast from the toaster, to change the coffee grounds.

So now the food is cooking itself.

While Marc is writing his poetry, eggs are finding the grill, frying, and flipping themselves over. Home fries are cooking up to a lovely crispness, and no matter how long they are left on the griddle, they never burn. Biscuits are showing up in pans in the oven, fluffy and hot and brushed with melted butter. Hamburgers are finding buns and lettuce, and french fries are finding oil.

Marc is writing fast, writing frantically, on anything he can find—napkins, customer bills, boxes of straws, anything. And, being the only person in the kitchen, he hasn't realized that he is not actually *cooking* all of the meals that are appearing on plates in the Van Gogh Cafe.

It is only when the lemon meringue pies start showing up that anyone notices what is happening. Clara notices. She realizes that her father is not the one doing the cooking, that lemon meringue pies are beyond him, and she considers saying something about it. But she is so *fond* of lemon meringue pies, and she is afraid they will disappear if she tells Marc he isn't the one who is baking them.

So she waits. She eats a lot of pie and she waits. Something else is bound to happen eventually.

And it does:

> So still and blue
> waiting
> waiting
> it is a long silver night

This is the poem Marc writes on a napkin that finds its way to Karla Roker's table. Karla has stopped in for a piece of pie on her way to visit her boyfriend in the next town. She reads the poem on the napkin, looks puzzled, smiles. She wipes the pie off her face and heads on out to her blue truck. It is about eight, just getting dark.

And at eleven, when Karla has spent nearly two hours stranded between Flowers and the next town over because her blue truck has broken down beside Silver Lake, when she sits waiting for a tow truck to come and remembers the poem on the napkin, then the bigger story begins.

Marc's poems are telling the future.

The back of Judy Jones's bill for a grilled cheese and Coke on Monday reads,

> Yellow and full
> did you know
> it would be spring

and on Tuesday her neighbor gives her a bouquet of daffodils for her birthday.

In the corner of a menu handed to Mary Showers, who has come in for lunch with her mother, a poem reads,

> Rain
> finds a sweetheart
> in the music

The following day, a boy in the record store asks Mary on a date.

And then the real magic happens. The magic Clara was waiting for.

One morning a young boy comes into the

cafe. He is fighting back tears. He asks if anyone has seen his Siamese cat, who has been lost for three days.

Today is a school holiday, so Clara is working. She hasn't seen the cat, and she feels terrible for the boy. She offers him a piece of lemon meringue pie, free, and tells him she will ask the other customers about the cat while he eats.

The boy sits quietly at a table, slowly eating the pie, as Clara goes to every person in the cafe, hoping. But no one has seen the Siamese. They are all very sorry about it.

Clara returns to the boy and sadly shakes her head. He has finished his pie and is about to thank her and go when he glances over at the SOUP TODAY board. Under Chicken Noodle, he reads,

> Blackberries love
> a moon-faced man
> so sleepy

The boy stops in his tracks and reads the board over and over. Then he tells Clara the name of his cat: *Blackberry.* Clara tells the customer sitting at the next table and that customer tells the next and before long the whole cafe is looking at the soup board. Some of them have already read their futures on napkins or menus. They know what they are seeing.

The Van Gogh Cafe is silent. All eyes are on the board and everyone is thinking, *Where is a moon-faced man in Flowers, Kansas?*

Then someone whispers, "The motel." Yes.

There is only one motel in Flowers, and it is not a very good one, but it does have a lovely name that has fooled a lot of tourists who reserved their rooms sight unseen. It is called Moonlight Manor.

And its sign beside the highway shows a round, sleepy moon, eyes closed, mouth smiling, little hearts flying all around.

The motel is a good three miles from the cafe. So someone gives the boy a ride. And in the ivy planter beneath the Moonlight Manor sign, Blackberry is sleeping. Her leg has been hurt, but she is all right. The boy cries and cries; he is so happy.

The next day at the Van Gogh Cafe everyone is buzzing. They know for sure now that Marc's poems are omens. Fortunes. Signs. What will his next one say?

But the speculation about omens doesn't last long. It is being replaced by complaints. Frank Mills has been waiting twenty minutes for his eggs. When they finally arrive, they're runny. Kathleen Cooper's pancakes are cold. Winston Fuller's steak is tough as leather. And there's not one lemon meringue pie in sight.

Food has stopped cooking itself, Marc has stopped writing poetry, and everyone's hat is staying on his head. Things are back to normal.

Clara is naturally a little disappointed, especially about the pies. It's back to plain old apple now.

But she won't be disappointed long. Lemon meringue pies can be lovely. But they're nothing compared to magic muffins. . . .

Magic Muffins

IN OCTOBER a woman dressed all in lace and pearls walks into the Van Gogh Cafe, fresh off I-70. She is traveling east to New York City to live in a loft. Clara thinks the woman is quite glamorous, and she feels shy around her.

At the moment, the woman is the cafe's only customer, and she holds a large straw bag close to her as she sips her 7Up. Marc has wandered out of the kitchen now and is starting up the phonograph, to give the place some life. Clara sits at the counter, working a crossword puzzle.

When the glamorous woman finishes her soft drink, she stands at the register to pay. The porcelain hen is smiling at her, and someone is singing that she would be so nice to come home to, and the combination of these things makes her feel generous. She brings forth from her straw bag a dollar for the bill plus a little foil package.

Then, easily as she came, the woman drives away to New York, leaving behind two magic muffins on the counter of the Van Gogh Cafe.

The muffins are inside the little foil package, of course, which Marc has unwrapped. Tiny muffins, gumdrop muffins, they are charming. Marc puts one in Clara's hand and one in his own.

"Like shells," Clara says.

Marc nods. He is still a little dreamy, thinking about the glamorous woman all in lace and pearls.

"May we eat them?" asks Clara.

Marc has a sudden intuition. He says to Clara, "Only if we first make a wish."

Well, a wish can be a blessing and a wish can be a curse, and Clara has read enough fairy tales to respect this. All at once she doesn't want the muffin.

Her caution makes Marc so nervous that all at once he isn't so sure he wants his, either. Not with a wish attached, anyway.

Soberly, they fold the muffins back into the foil and slide the little package into the refrigerator and stop thinking about wishes.

But magic doesn't have to be eaten in order to work. It needs only to be believed. And when Clara and Marc put the little foil package away, there is no stronger proof of belief than this. And now a new story in the Van Gogh Cafe is unfolding.

The next day Clara is so curious. She wants to see the muffins again. They are only muffins, tiny gifts from a glamorous woman. But now the wishing business has turned them into so much more.

Clara unwraps the foil.

She should have known. She should have known all along.

The muffins *are* magic. Because now there are three.

She doesn't tell Marc. He seems to have forgotten all about the muffins anyway. Clara loves waiting for things to happen, waiting and watching secretly. She folds up the foil and is still.

And the next day, there are four muffins.

The next, five.

The next, six.

The next, seven.

Every day Clara unwraps the foil to find a tiny new muffin. And every day she folds the package up again and slides it to the back of the refrigerator.

Clara knows something is about to happen.

And when November arrives, exactly twelve days after the woman in lace and pearls has passed through the Van Gogh Cafe, something does: Kansas is hit with one of the all-time biggest snowstorms in its history.

No one is prepared. They've barely folded away their Halloween costumes. Snow shovels are lying down in their basements somewhere. Boots are at the bottom of old trunks. Nobody's had a chance to get a new pair of gloves at Kmart. Goodness knows there's no salt for the front steps.

And on this day of one of the biggest snowstorms in Kansas history, there is a church bus traveling down the road. The bus is full of small children, children not yet old enough for school, children just big enough to spend two hours at the church molding Play-Doh while their mothers shop.

26

This bus is taken by surprise in the freak Kansas blizzard. It has no chains, no snow tires. It hasn't a chance of staying on the road. It slides and hits a pole, one-half mile from the Van Gogh Cafe.

The sheriff and his deputies arrive. Firemen. Anyone who can make it through the snow is at the bus, lifting out crying children. There are fourteen of them, small and cold and scared. Some have bumped their mouths or their heads and these cry loudest.

The snow falls so fast and thick and deep that there is no getting them to the county hospital, which is a good ten miles away. So when that's ruled out, the first place everyone thinks of is the Van Gogh Cafe.

The children are carried into the cafe, and they do not look well. Marc and Clara help settle them into booths and onto chairs, and the children's faces are gray, their fingers blue. They are alarmingly quiet.

And now the true magic starts.

Because Clara, counting all of the children, has seen that there are fourteen of them. And she knows, for she has already looked this morning, that there are fourteen tiny muffins in that little foil package in the refrigerator.

And Clara understands now why the muffins are so small.

Marc and the rest of the adults are trying to get the children to sip some coffee. It is the only hot drink already made.

But these are tiny children. They will not take coffee.

What they will take, what they do take, are tiny muffins. Clara moves from one child to the next, the foil package in her hand, and into each little mouth she places a muffin.

And one by one, the children become warm and alive again. Their fingers no longer hurt. Their faces are full of color. Their bruises disappear. Their cuts heal. No one's head aches. And not one tooth is missing.

Clara drops the empty foil into the trash can.

When, for many days after, Clara and her father speak of the blizzard and of the magic muffins, they have no regrets about the wish they each passed up. Clara regrets only that she didn't tell Marc about the multiplying muffins sooner, for he loves the mystery of it. He loves to hear her story.

But young girls need secrets now and then. Secrets are like pieces of silver.

And besides, someone with a deeper secret is about to arrive at the Van Gogh Cafe. Some-one tall and sad and elegant. Someone who could be a star . . .

The Star

I T IS NEARLY Christmas now, and the Van Gogh Cafe is luminous. Old-fashioned tree lights are strung all around the door, and candy canes hang everywhere. Each customer takes a candy cane when he leaves. Small paper antlers have been glued onto the porcelain hen's head, and over ALL DOGS someone has taped SANTA. BLESS SANTA. The phonograph has changed its tune—the only time of year a different record is played—and Nat King Cole is singing "Silent Night."

Outside it's cold. A winter wind in Kansas gets going and there's nothing to stop it. A little breeze can kick up in the east and in a matter of minutes have people shivering two hundred miles to the west. Wind loves a flat land.

So the customers are especially grateful for Marc's strong, hot coffee and the warmth that makes the cafe windows moist with perspiration.

Christmas, of course, simply enhances the cafe's magic, its mystery. And in December, in early morning, the Van Gogh Cafe is a fine place to meet someone you haven't seen in a long, long time.

There aren't many new faces in the cafe this season, given the weather, so the man is noticed the moment he walks in. He is tall and slender, and he moves like water. Besides being strikingly handsome, he is a fabulous dresser. Black cloak, black cashmere scarf, black wool gloves, a black cane.

His white hair sets it all off perfectly. He must be ninety years old.

Clara is filling up napkin holders when he walks in. She looks up and meets his eyes, and at once she feels he knows everything about her.

The Van Gogh Cafe brings out the best in people, so though all the customers are full of curiosity, no one stares at this man. A few smile briefly as he makes his way to the small back table by the window. Then they return to themselves.

Clara continues filling the holders as one of the waitresses takes the elegant man's order: "Tea, plain. A boiled egg, please. Thank you." He has a lovely voice. Lovely manners. Clara thinks there is something so romantic about him.

Marc comes out of the kitchen. He is looking for his watch, which he believes he put inside the porcelain hen (her head lifts off), and as he looks around the cafe to smile and greet his customers, Marc suddenly sees the elegant man at the small back table. And unlike everyone else who has remembered his good manners, Marc stops what he is doing and stares.

The man smiles shyly and looks away.

Marc is staring because he knows who this is. He looks around the cafe to see if anyone else realizes who is among them. No one does. No one remembers this man's movies.

But Marc remembers them all. Marc has seen all of the old silent films, the ones with Charles Chaplin and Mary Pickford and Douglas Fairbanks. He knows them by heart, and he knows the actors' faces like he knows his daughter's face, and Marc is *certain* who this elegant man in the cafe is.

He is a star.

Clara doesn't know, of course. She has watched old movies with her father, but, except for Chaplin, she doesn't know the actors. Only their movements.

And it is perhaps the way the elegant man has moved through the cafe that reminds her of something she has seen before. Reminds everyone. But none can quite place the memory.

The breakfast hours pass and people go their way, to work, to the mall at the edge of town, back home to put up a tree.

But the elegant man stays on. He has hardly touched his egg. His teacup is still half full. The door of the Van Gogh Cafe opens and closes, opens and closes, and he stays on, looking out the window.

Marc cannot help himself. When there is no one left in the cafe except the silent star, Marc walks over to his table. Clara, curious, shyly follows.

Marc offers his hand and the man gracefully takes it. They shake.

"I know your work," Marc says softly. "I love it. I love all your films."

Clara's eyes are wide. She has not known until now that a star is in her cafe.

The old man blushes and smiles.

"Thank you," he says.

There is an awkward moment, then, graciously, he offers Marc and Clara the two empty chairs at his table.

Happily, they sit.

Marc and the silent star talk about the old films as Clara listens. There is an innocence in her father's face she has not seen before. He is like a boy. The silent star seems pleased, quietly thrilled, to talk of his work with someone who understands so well. He laughs and sighs and even trembles slightly, reliving it all.

There is a moment or two when each is quiet, catching his breath.

"Why, sir, are you at the Van Gogh Cafe?" Marc gently asks. Clara waits.

The old man seems glad someone has asked. He reaches into his coat and pulls forth an old photograph. He hands it first to Clara, then to Marc.

It is of a beautiful young man in a waistcoat and top hat, standing before an old theater. Marc looks carefully at the building in the picture.

"Is this . . . ?"

"Yes," replies the silent star.

The building is the Van Gogh Cafe. In 1923. When it was a theater.

"He and I did some shows here together, the summer we met." The silent star smiles and puts the photograph back inside his coat.

"Today I am waiting for him," he says.

Clara's heart is pounding. She feels that she herself is in a movie. Every gesture the man makes, each word he speaks is so beautiful to her. She knows the cafe remembers this man. She can feel it drawing in to him, reaching for this man who has been a part of its first magic, on the stage of the old theater.

Oddly, not one person has walked into the cafe to break this spell.

Marc offers the star a fresh cup of tea and a piece of apple pie, which is gratefully accepted. Then Marc and Clara leave the old man to his waiting.

The lunch hours come and go. Then the dinner hours. The silent star waits. Occasionally Clara or Marc offer him something, but he politely declines. And they find themselves watching the window, watching the door, for a beautiful young man in a top hat and waistcoat.

Finally, it is time to close and still the old man is waiting. He seems very tired now. But unworried. He asks Marc if he might sit by the window a little longer.

"Of course," says Marc, though he offers his guest room to the man, offers to take him home for the evening and return him to the table by the window the next day.

But the man is certain his friend is coming very soon.

"Very soon," he says.

So Marc takes Clara home and returns to the cafe a few hours later, to check on the old man.

At first Marc thinks the man is asleep. Then Marc realizes that he has died.

In the old man's hand, Marc finds a newspaper clipping, cracked and yellow. The clipping shows the face of the beautiful young man in top hat and waistcoat. It reports that he has drowned, in 1926.

And in the old man's other hand is the same photograph that Marc and Clara were shown. But now the photograph is changed. The beautiful young man is gone, and there is only a soft empty light where he was standing.

Marc and Clara keep the photograph and the newspaper clipping inside a small box near the cash register, and on Christmas Eve when everything is quiet, they look at these again. They each think how perfect that the silent star has died where he found his true love. That he came to the Van Gogh Cafe and waited for his friend to take him home.

But the star will not be the last wanderer making his way home by way of the Van Gogh Cafe. There will be others. In fact, one is about to land on its roof.

Magic is never wasted on a wayward gull. . . .

The Wayward Gull

EVERYONE KNEW when the seagull arrived at the Van Gogh Cafe because as soon as it got there it robbed Bill Waters. Bill had just finished lunch and was out on the sidewalk, sticking a dollar bill into his wallet, when the gull swooped down, plucked the bill right out of his hand, and ate it. People said the gull must have heard some mother say to her child, "Here's a dollar for lunch," and gotten all mixed-up.

So now it is February and there is a seagull living on the Van Gogh Cafe. This is odd even for the people of Flowers, who have grown used to strangeness. But there is a gull on the roof, beside the oven vent, and everyone is having to adjust.

Of course, Clara loves having a gull.

After she heard about Bill Waters, she went out on the sidewalk and fluttered a dollar bill around a few times, hoping to bring the gull down. It didn't work. But when she fluttered a few french fries, the gull showed up right away. Evidently the money hadn't agreed with it. But it loved the fries.

So each day now Clara is feeding the gull. She has become quite fond of it. And the people of Flowers have gotten used to having a seagull in town. Things are almost beginning to feel normal.

But there is a cat across the street. And magic is about to happen.

The cat belongs to Linda Everly, who owns a nice used-paperback bookshop across from the cafe. The cat's name is Emerald, and she has been living in Flowers for nine years without ever seeing a gull.

And now she has seen one.

Clara is the first to notice Emerald's new hobby. Clara is filling up the ketchup bottles in the cafe when she looks out the window and sees Emerald carrying someone's mitten in her mouth. Clara smiles at Emerald and goes back to her work. She doesn't understand yet what is happening.

But the next day she sees Emerald crossing the street, trailing a long scarf, and Clara begins to wonder if maybe some magic is starting.

And when the following day she sees Emerald lugging someone's snow boot across the road, Clara is certain there is magic going on.

Clara walks outside the cafe to see where Emerald has taken the boot. She looks up and down the sidewalk, over by the trash cans, down the alley. Nothing. Then she hears a happy cry and a meow.

Clara steps back until she can see the roof of the cafe and the oven vent where the gull is living. And there sits the gull, the cat, and about ten mittens, five scarves, three mismatched boots, and a sock.

Emerald is in love.

Clara brings her father out to see the pair on the roof, and as they are standing there, watching romance happen, somebody else comes along, and somebody else, and somebody else until there are about twenty people standing in front of the Van Gogh Cafe, looking up. This is enough to attract a photographer from the *Flowers Gazette*, and she snaps a picture of the seagull, the cat, and the winter apparel.

The photograph appears in the *Gazette* the next day, and somebody from the Associated Press sees it and puts it on the wire service, and the next thing you know, Emerald's love-happy face is in newspapers all across the country. Just because she brought some warm clothing to a seagull in Kansas.

Soon after, cameras are filling up the Van Gogh Cafe and Clara and Marc are on national TV.

Once this happens, letters begin to arrive at the Van Gogh Cafe from all over the country. They are coming to the cafe by the hundreds. And what most of the letters are asking for is a feather from the gull because people believe the gull is an angel and that its feathers will bring them good luck.

Well, of course, Clara and Marc aren't about to pluck feathers from their gull. They wouldn't do it under any circumstances, but they especially won't do it in February when a gull needs all the feathers it can get.

Still, the letters trouble them, for they

think their gull might be in some danger. And they are right.

One night as Marc is working late, baking pies for the next day, he hears a scuffling overhead. When he goes outside, he sees a dark figure on the cafe roof, grabbing at the gull, which is flapping in the air just above the oven vent.

Marc yells and the intruder slides down the back of the roof and runs off into the night.

The gull settles itself again beside the warm vent, and Marc returns to the cafe. Worried.

Things get worse. Every few days or so, Marc sees someone new in town, lurking around his cafe. He has a bad feeling about these people. And so does Emerald, for she has lost all interest in romancing the gull. She stays in the bookshop where a cat is safe.

Marc doesn't say anything to Clara about the bad feeling and the strangers in Flowers. He doesn't want to worry her.

But of course Clara knows. Clara watches everything. She has been watching these people and she doesn't like them and she wants them to go away. Clara knows there is only one way to make them go.

So every time she goes outside with a french fry in her hand, she tells the gull as it swoops down, "Go to California." Three or four times a day: "Go to California."

The letters are pouring in and strangers are lurking and things are not right at all at the Van Gogh Cafe. Clara wonders where its magic has gone as she and Marc put the twentieth bag of letters in the alley beside the back door.

But sometimes magic takes a little while longer to get where it's going. Especially in February, when the weather can slow anybody down.

Clara need not have doubted the cafe. For real magic is on its way. In fact, it is landing right now.

It is about 5:00 on Thursday afternoon when Clara sees the first gull; 5:03 when she sees the second; 5:05 when she sees the third. And by 6:00, fifty new seagulls are sitting on the roof of the Van Gogh Cafe.

Everybody in Flowers passes by and just shakes his head. They are all getting used to this.

Yet Clara knows that magic is the reason for the gulls. She waits to see what will happen next as Marc just wanders about the cafe, more worried than ever.

By closing time nothing has happened, except for a lot of squawking. Clara and Marc lock up and go home.

But the following morning, something *has* happened. Something wonderful.

The gulls have eaten all twenty bags of mail that were sitting by the back door. All those crazy letters from people wanting a gull feather are gone, and there are fifty-one fat, happy gulls on the roof.

47

Marc's spirits are high. Clara's faith is restored. And then comes more.

At about 4:30, a big U-Haul truck pulls in front of the cafe. Two young women step out of it and come in for some coffee. They are traveling west on I-70, and it is good to have a break from sitting in that truck, they say. They relax and drink their coffee.

And as the women sit, Clara looks out the window and sees a gull fly down and land on top of their truck. Then she sees another. And another. And within minutes, every gull from the Van Gogh Cafe is on top of the U-Haul truck, waiting for the women to finish their coffee.

When the women do, they go outside and there are fifty-one birds sitting on their truck, looking at them. Well, what are you going to do when a gull wants a ride? You're going to give it to him.

So the women shrug their shoulders,

climb into the truck, and back it out onto the road.

And as they are pulling away, Clara, who is still standing at the window, sees the side of the truck for the first time.

On it is a picture of someone surfing in the ocean. It says: CALIFORNIA. AMERICA'S MOVING ADVENTURE.

This is some of the best magic Clara has ever seen at the Van Gogh Cafe. She watches the birds drive away and knows that Marc's bad feeling will disappear and no more strangers will be lurking, and the cafe can rest awhile from all the excitement.

For the next couple of months the phonograph will softly play, the hen will smile, dogs will be blessed, and things will be just perfect by the time the door opens and in walks the writer.

The Writer

E HAS BEEN trying to be a writer for four years. It isn't that he isn't any good at writing. Most people say he is quite good.

But publishers just don't seem to like his work. They want him to make his stories simpler, so people don't have to think too much while they are reading. And they would like him to add more excitement, perhaps make someone jump off a bridge. They tell the writer he doesn't have enough beautiful women and enough beautiful men. They ask him if he's ever thought about writing a diet book. Diet books sell very well, they say.

All of this has, of course, made the writer quite poor, and if ever anyone didn't need to think about dieting, it is he. He has been living on brown rice and lettuce for a long time.

What is he doing in Flowers, Kansas, in early spring?

The writer is on his way to the Pacific to see the gray whales. He gave up writing, and instead delivered telephone directories until he had enough money to drive to Oregon.

So here he is, in the Van Gogh Cafe.

He sits peacefully at a table and watches everything around him. The young man who owns the cafe, Marc, interests him. Marc has his long hair in a ponytail and today is wearing a shirt that reads YES. Just that. YES. Marc seems happy in his cafe. Now and then he pats something affectionately. The phonograph, the hen, the pie carousel, his daughter.

The daughter fascinates the writer. She is so still. Wide, watchful eyes. She reminds him of the moon or an owl. Her brown hair is braided down her back and she wears a sunflower jumper and basketball shoes. She has noticed the writer and from time to time she glances at him. Curious. He loves her curiosity.

The writer sits a long time watching people come and go. He watches their faces change when they enter the Van Gogh Cafe— the tiredness lift, the worry relax, the hurry slow down. They come in and they are kind and modest and funny.

The writer understands now the song playing on the old phonograph.

And as he sits, the magic in those walls begins its work on him. There in the Van Gogh Cafe, he is reminded of what he is and of what he finds beautiful. His heart swells with the revelation that he is a real writer and not meant to deliver telephone directories or produce diet books. He remembers that the artist for whom this cafe is named sold only one painting in his entire life. And the writer knows that he has a book inside him. But he isn't sure what to call it.

When he finally decides to get back on the road to Oregon, he walks up to the register to pay his bill. The hen smiles at him. Marc tells him, "Have a good trip."

And as he leaves, the writer looks over at Clara who is quietly reading. He can't see the title of her book because the neon sign in the cafe window is reflecting across the jacket, making a new title.

It is calling the book *The Van Gogh Cafe*.

And that is all the writer needed to know.

Developmental Studies Center (DSC) is a nonprofit, mission-driven educational publisher. Since 1980, we have created research-based programs that build students' academic skills while simultaneously facilitating their social, emotional, and ethical development. Our mission is to provide schools with innovative curricula that motivate students to grow as readers, writers, and members of their communities.

Authentic literature is at the heart of our literacy programs. Children's books are deeply interwoven into every lesson, either in a read-aloud or as part of individual student work. Rich, multicultural fiction and nonfiction bring the full range of human experience and knowledge into the classroom.

Engaged teachers facilitate the exchange of student ideas in DSC classrooms. These conversations spark curiosity and a desire to participate in the learning process that reaps benefits far beyond the immediate goals of learning to read and write. Combining quality curricula and great literature enriches the educational experience for all students and teachers.

We would like to express our thanks to Houghton Mifflin Harcourt Publishing Company for allowing us to reprint this book.

DEVELOPMENTAL STUDIES CENTER

Educating Minds and Hearts™